New *Love* Poems

New Love Poems

Terry Benczik

BALBOA.
PRESS

A DIVISION OF HAY HOUSE

Balboa Press books may be ordered through booksellers or by contacting:

Balboa Press
A Division of Hay House
1663 Liberty Drive
Bloomington, IN 47403
www.balboapress.com
1-(877) 407-4847

Because of the dynamic nature of the Internet, any web addresses or links contained in this book may have changed since publication and may no longer be valid. The views expressed in this work are solely those of the author and do not necessarily reflect the views of the publisher, and the publisher hereby disclaims any responsibility for them.

The author of this book does not dispense medical advice or prescribe the use of any technique as a form of treatment for physical, emotional, or medical problems without the advice of a physician, either directly or indirectly. The intent of the author is only to offer information of a general nature to help you in your quest for emotional and spiritual well-being. In the event you use any of the information in this book for yourself, which is your constitutional right, the author and the publisher assume no responsibility for your actions.

Any people depicted in stock imagery provided by Thinkstock are models, and such images are being used for illustrative purposes only. Certain stock imagery © Thinkstock.

ISBN: 978-1-4525-7521-6 (sc)
ISBN: 978-1-4525-7522-3 (hc)
ISBN: 978-1-4525-7523-0 (e)

Library of Congress Control Number: 2013909671

Printed in the United States of America.

Balboa Press rev. date: 8/12/2013

Dedication

To Kindness, Compassion, Mercy, and to All That Is Love.

Acknowledgements

Thank you, my dear friend, S.P.M. You have been the perfect guide for this amazing experience called life.

Photography by William Vandever. www.williamvandevercamerawork.com

Special thanks to Kenneth P. Borbet for your thoughtful editorial comments and your supportive friendship.

Special thanks to Colin Dexter for your translation of the title in the poem "Quietum Est Mare Profundum," and for your encouragement.

Great love and appreciation to Helene Benczik and Diane Benczik.

With deep gratitude to "Team Terry" for your generous support in every way. Many thanks to: Meg Anzalone, Diana Boycheck, Bill Cahill, Irene & Mike Charney, Michele Cuomo, Darlene Danielsen, Robert Dannenmann, Laurel Davis, Donald Dudley, Jayne Howard Feldman, Sylvia Gonzalez, W. R. Goode, Dr. William Hawes, Martha Hayden, Alan Hicks, Coleen Hopson, Leigh Kapps, Kris Kearns, Carole Kirby, Kathy Kovach, Ann Krupski, Christine Kwiatkowski, Maria Malone-Hodges, Frank Marsella, Marilyn Mattei, Joseph McGrann, Dr. Mark Pasmantier, Gitanjali Patel, Manuel Peraza, Deborah Rosenstock, Rosie Sabo, Joan Short, The Sisters at the Spiritual Center, Harry Smith, Faith & Harvey Spitz, Howe Stidger, Dana Srebrenick, Keith Thacker, The TRD Group (P.A.), Ronnie Urs, William Vandever, Maria Varga, and Ginger Wolpert. Thanks to all who prayed or who helped me on the journey.

Table of Contents

Chapter One

---~~~∽◦✿◦∽~~~---

Attraction

On Seeing Stewart Granger
in a Deli on 57th Street

A royal prince walked in;
(He must have been!)
so stunning, my jaw dropped,
and everything in the deli
literally stopped.
The manager marched over.
"Sir, do I know you?
You look familiar . . ."
And he, smile bemused,
hair of silver, said,
"I was an actor . . .
a swashbuckler . . ."
Then, in his best
pirate stance,
he smiled at the gawpers
circled around him
while making a fencing
gesture in the air with his hand.
No one who was in line to get
their sand-
wiches thought about food.
I wanted to break into applause
and congratulate him
for all he was.
Instead, there was a quiet
bow, invisible somehow.
All we could do was stare.
New Yorkers, yes.
But he was magnificent—
confident.

A rare thing.
So graceful, so present.
I have never seen such
polish and élan.
He was soon given his takeaway
and was gone.
And though I'm not a fan
of his film chronology,
I say this now
without apology.
Sometimes, when I'm missing glamour
or I'm bored,
I think of the day
of the splendid swashbuckler
and his sword.

British actor Stewart Granger was primarily cast in romantic and heroic film roles, including numerous costume dramas. His popularity was greatest from the 1940s to the 1960s. Mr. Granger wielded a sword in films such as *The Prisoner of Zenda*, *The Swordsman of Siena*, and *Moonfleet*.

What I Really Wanted to Say Instead of "Hello"

Your eyes are so big
and so *blue*
I could go swimming
in them on a hot
summer's day
and never leave.

Your Beautiful Face

I remember calling my best friend
and telling her I had feelings for you—
a crush, probably—
but I was certain I had feelings for you.

The embarrassing thing is
I couldn't recall the color of your eyes,
whether you wore glasses, or
even the shade of your hair.

I remembered your laugh,
your kindness, your gentleness,
and the sound of your voice.
But the rest—I was panicked!

I never really looked at you as if you
were in the swimsuit competition for
Mr. America. I did remember that
definitely, probably, you might be
taller than me.

I had known you for a little while, and yet
the only truth I knew about you was you.

I am charmed by you, the sum of your parts,
and it is not about your nose or the angle
of your cheekbones.

My best friend reassured me (the way best friends do),
"You really *do* care for him. Your soul *sees* him.
Calm down; breathe deep. There's a chance he sees
who you are, too."

But, she advised me (the way best friends do),
"When you run into him, it's okay to take
a good, long look and enjoy the scenery."

So next time I meet you,
I can't wait to see your beautiful face
for the very first time.

Dreams of Discovery

There is that Lana Turner part of us
that sits, with hair perfect, and cosmetics
freshly applied, waiting in the Sweet Shoppe
at the luncheon counter
to be discovered by a famous magician
who will make our dreams come true.

Waiting for someone who truly sees us,
who sees we are so amazing,
the whole world must be informed.
Who knows it is nothing
to do with our appearance. Who sees the
indescribable *it* that no one else owns.

I am The Wizard concealed. I see your beauty,
and I want to bring light to all that makes you
sparkle in my eyes.
These things take time.

Be patient, that Lana Turner part of you.
This sorcerer is careful, and your specialness
is sublime. I must pretend not to see it
in spite of myself. That way, we may allow room
for the real magic to happen.

Lana Turner was a well-known movie actress who was discovered as a teen while drinking a cola at a soda fountain in Hollywood. Unlike other actresses who have had to endure years of struggle for recognition, Ms. Turner's path to stardom seemed predestined.

Chapter Two

Excitement

Ruminations on Love

Savaged by love,
Destroyed by love,
Ripped apart by love,
My insides scooped out by love.
Whipped by love,
Enslaved by love,
Tortured by love,
Torn and shredded by love,
Elevated by love,
Lightened by love,
Time and time again, fooled by love.
Abandoned by love,
Flirted with by love,
Left all bubbly and giggling by love.
Boosted by love,
Buoyed by love.
Held afloat by love in a storm.
Pieced together by love.
Loved by love.
Oh, love, what are you?
Oh, love, who are you?

Whoever, whatever the love is for,
it is the same feeling:
exalted, bigger than
anything else in the whole world.
Oh, love. I see you now.
I know you now.
I am love.

Oceanography

Sea-calm,
hungry shark,
always moving,
sleek and firm.
Some days, tuna;
some days, caviar.
Thirst never slaked,
appetite never satisfied
in an ocean
filled with food.
That's what I feel when I kiss you.

The threat
of teeth.
A splash
of cologne.
Wild desire.
I will
be consumed
like shimmering
bait.

Coral reef,
feeding frenzy.
An adrenaline
surge that
races the
pulse.
That's what I feel when I kiss you.
That's why I'll kiss you again.

A Dangerous Poem

This dangerous, dangerous poem
with points so sharp, you could cut
your fingers on the pages.

It's too adult for children to read
and could upset far too many people
with the wrong thing on their minds.

This poem is so dangerous, only the most
trusted may view it.

It has the potential to awaken grave emotions
long buried!
To make the dishonorable repent their sins.

Yet it could wreak havoc in quarters I seek
to protect.

You see, this dangerous poem could cause you to
realize the extent of my hidden feelings for you.
That's more risk than I have ever wanted to take.

For You, My Love

Cast my fate with you?
You tormented fellow.
I love you for all of your faults.
You love me too much to see
these faults are shared.

Expose me to the light? Don't!
Too much sunlight fades everything.
Keep us secret.

I'll be your sweet inner whisper,
the faraway look in your eye,
the person you talk to when alone in the car.
I was a good sleeper till I met you.
Now I sit bolt upright in bed at odd hours,
feeling your distant thoughts travel far and fast
and kiss me awake.

It's ridiculous to love you.
But we are both fools for love.
I have known nothing
that compares to this.
So let our story begin.

Complicated

My love for you is not complicated.
It's a glass that's overflowing.
You say you love me
so much,
you are scared
to go forward.
Where do we put all these feelings?
You're afraid *it* won't last?
What won't?
Dive into the water.
Love is not complicated.
It's love.
Happiness is a choice,
not a far and distant land.

The Letter

My heart leaps,
and I rush to the door,
insert my key,
hear the satisfying click.
Inside, I wash my hands,
a purifying ritual;
I want to come to you clean.

Then I run my finger
under the lip
of the envelope
your own hand has addressed,
your own mouth has sealed.

I feel the lightweight papers
in between my fingers
and look intently
for any impression that
you wish to give me.

I put the pages
back inside—
where your hands have been,
where your lips has been—
and lightly hold the envelope
and smile.

Letters are such satisfying things.
Such intimate things.
I would not feel
the same way about you
if all you did was text message.

A Fleeting Feeling

Let me live inside this kiss.
You are turmoil and remorse and regret
and a longing for things of times past.
You analyze everything.
You think too much, you read too much,
you feel too much. I want every bit.

Lost

I was driving,
and I got lost.

Lost in your town.
Lost in the place of you.
Lost in the thought of you.
Lost in the eyes of you.
Lost in the you of you.

Lost.

I knew I was going somewhere,
but my heart took its own direction.
Lost, but not alone.

Chapter Three

Frustration

Office Routine

Woman answers phone, lengthily, officiously, with
her name, her title, company name, and the
ever-polite, "May I help you?"
Then she transfers the call
to the correct extension and whispers,
"Darn, wasted my sexy voice again!"

Sea Stories

Land and sky both meet the sea,
but all three seem to love equally.

Ocean pours its soul upon the land,
endlessly touching glistening sand.

The sky is shy and meets the deep,
quietly and softly, save when it will weep.

Yet whom does the ocean love the best—
the pulse of the earth held in her breast,

or the thundering skies that make her rise
and fall that her heart does call?

Land and sky both meet the sea,
but all three seem to love equally:

the sea, the earth, the expanse of sky,
they all have bigger hearts than I.

The River

An ancient soothsayer told me
in another life,
I was a Chinese boy
whose twin brother married well.
I was not content.
There was a special girl;
yet my time was spent
waiting for the right moment
to speak of my intentions.
One day, I discovered
the girl I loved was taken
to a village far in the north.
My heart was on fire,
and I found myself cursing fate for
bringing you to a place
I could never even imagine.
I travelled for days
and soon grew hungry, finding little food.
Hearing news of you in the wind,
I journeyed to a powerful river
that lay between us.
Tired and not a good swimmer,
the river put out the light
inside of me.
In this life,
I face that river
over and over
to try and get to you.
When will this journey end in happiness?

A Low, Mean Wind

A low, mean wind
pulls off of the water
and touches my face
just enough
to catch me off-guard.

Like a lover's hand
brushing against my ear
it reminds me
my body has been
in a long, vacant sleep.

This low, mean wind
it flutters and stirs
and makes me
sometimes feel that
I cannot control
anything that matters.

It's Time To Get Real

A
crumb
is
not
a
A crumb is not a meal.
is not
a meal.

Any Word?

Hung up on you
But what to do?
For you are the riddle
and I don't have a clue.
So much time
spent waiting for your call
spent waiting for any word
from you at all.
Is it wise?
I analyze
your words, your deeds?
They all seem so tiny
when weighed against my needs.
Ages go by
until I hear
it's only been weeks
It feels like a year.
I'm glib, I'm funny
it's so absurd

You secretly know
I hang on every word.

I hang on every word.
Every word and excuse
You braid pretty words
And tighten my noose.
I hang on your every word.

All this for wanting
a few strings attached
I'm stuck in a web
I'm not sure who's thatched
I try to guess your angle
but mostly—I just dangle
I hang on your every word.

<u>Just So You Get the Point</u>
I hang on your every word.

Chapter Four

Hurt & Despair

Anthem for William

Not all pain is exquisite
nor suffering special.
Some is of the mundane variety.
The knowledge, for example,
that the same monotonous days
are destined to repeat
without love
without hope
without blessed human contact
or the special bonds
which restore dreams
open floodgates
allow light to pour in.
Not all yearning is of the highest
order-
that which leads
to some magical conclusion.
Some types hide neatly in your pocket
and so close to the heart
are never mentioned
for fear
of ripping open hidden wounds.

Encounter with the Stellar

I held a brilliant shining star. It gleamed.
Its colors were amazing me. I dreamed.
It didn't care—it burnt my hand. I screamed.

Wild, Wild Woes

Drinking ruined everything in your family
It took your childhood,
destroyed your Father, turned your Mother
into martyr and saint but she loved her dear son.

We did try to get somewhere
but those half sweet half trouble—a kid's drink really
they made your slur and sputter and angry
that everything hurt and nothing was
ever any good.

Your Father damaged you by never even touching you.
That hollow pain, you cherish it you treasure it.
It is not myth and romance and telling stories all around—
a bonding thing between brothers of the barstool.

It's the futility of trying to feel nothing even though you're
alive. It attracts you more than a hundred dollar whore.
My birthday, your birthday, the birth of possibility,—
you'd spend half the night drinking and then come home
stinking and childlike and remembering the obscure—
as if I'd be happy to see you—like your Mother was.
I am not your Mother.

Your Father's drinking ruined everything.
But that was thirty years ago.
What ruins everything now?

A Twenty-Year-Old Girl
Rips-Up Your Valentine

For eight long months we fought.
We quarreled and chided.
There were days and walks
along verdant landscapes
drives in the country
and crumpled maps along the freeway.

I didn't expect to see her
balled-up on the carpet
on the floor of your new apartment.
Wispy hair, eyes, a nose.
A real live American Girl.
I could plainly see that
she was pretty as well.

I tried to react offhandedly
rattling about everything inconsequential
That flooded my brain.
Thinking back, you were no help
in the conversation.
Her answers were monosyllabic.
She was no villain.

And was clearly hurt, too.
but clammed up while I
talked about—anything.
I left quickly
secretly assuring myself
with thoughts like
"She's just some random girl,
I went to college at 16 . . .
And, anyway, I'll bet she never
won a poetry contest
In the tenth grade, like I did."

A hell of a lot of good
having won a poetry contest
does in situations like these.

Invocation to Freyja

Oh Goddess Freyja, what say you?
What part of Love do I not understand?
Your cry golden tears over loss.
Your husband, the God of Ecstasy
is with you no more.

The bravest, once defeated
seek you for comfort.
You are the muse
for transcendent love.
You can change wood into iron.

As you look out from your throne
at the edge of the
the Milky Way Galaxy
Please tell me how
to melt my heart of steel
and fill it with laughter again.

Blind Desire

I have a big picture window.
It lets me look out at the world.
Have you ever seen a bird try and fly through
a window pane, not realizing what's there?
With the stubbornness of more flighty characters
I keep hitting the clear wall
full impact
bent on getting through
to that place
where we once were happy
somewhere beyond the range
of all I survey
no matter how much it hurts
and no matter how much
being there makes no sense.
I've seen several birds try
to fly through the living room's solid portal.
They either strike so hard they die
or recover from the stun and fly away.
But there was one
angry at the obstacle
downed four times and
determined to try again.
I pulled the shade
and tried to wave her away.
She majestically took aim.
Quickly, loudly, with cracked glass
it was over.
I buried her somberly
astonished at her determination
and the futility of my love for you.

Past Tense

When we bumped
into each other last week
you said you had recently married.
You said it as if it were something
to throw at me.
It didn't hurt.

Be grateful I did not accept your gifts!

I did not put your heart in my basket
because there was a hole
where the branches were meant
to be woven together.

The heart wants what it . . .
But my heart was grieving and not
able to share my private wound.

You would not have felt comfort
or rest anywhere near it.
I don't understand how you imagined
you ever could.

Take your sweet wife to the islands,
and take many pictures.
I could not love you
and you turned that into a weapon
against yourself.
Go, go, go, and be happy already.
There's got to be a better system for all of this.

Regret

War and greed and hate and lust
all evil fades, as it must.
and those who live in sadder times
can mourn for what was left behind

Age's wisdom pays the price
long-seen debris from every vice
and what is cash or fame or fear
tis' only ash when memory's near

Some said in an embittered past
unrequited love's the kind that lasts
and they who live to seize the day
we do so in our awkward way

You were my love I trusted long
and you became my soul's sad song
for I've held others
who've loved much more
and yet it's you at my heart's core

This is a weeping of the soul
to gather strength and keep me whole
and at the end of this long life
I do not reflect on grief and strife

Yet if I should see
once more your face
It would be grace.
It would be grace.

A Tale of The Heart

Some voices just feel like home
like wave on water
like rain on the window
with the fireplace bright
the kettle just poured
all warm and cozy
and a good book waiting.

Some speech sounds like music
playing the complicated tune
you've always wanted to hear
and you recognize your anthem
in such a simple way
your heart cannot help but dance—
Gently describing the world
in such a charming manner
one can imagine the faeries circling round you
to hear a tender tale.

Your voice, a touch on my arm to calm me
the world seemed friendlier then
conquerable, too.

It must be foolish of me
to want what cannot be
to seek to return
to a home in the heart
I've only known for moments
and for eternity.
To want to hear those words
like a favorite recording
to lean against you in times of trouble
and know all will be well.

I'm older now
and a little bit nostalgic
still a romantic
and for past times—I bow to you.

But I've learned a bit
sometimes we cannot retrace our travels
and heart's home I must rebuild
and furnish to my liking
for the comfort that I seek
I must first find within.

Heeling

They say the heel of the loaf is
the worst part.
A man who is a heel is the dregs.
They call you a heel but
you're my Achilles' heel
mythological and great and calamitous.
My love, my ruin, my regret
and once
my dearest hope.

Some say we are defined
by our best parts.
I say also by our worst.
You are at the very heart of me
the part that failed me
the part I've accepted and forgiven.

When we look at the whole of
ourselves,
I can't say I love all parts the same.
But, inexplicably,
there's a tender spot for you.

Chapter Five

Thoughts

With Love to Grace Darling

"In a storm-tossed night upon the blackest sea
Grace Darling rowed her way into history
Seeing the crippled craft from the lighthouse nest
she saved their lives and by all England was blessed."

I do know some lives need saving, if you are in the path
of a meteor, or tied to a railroad track, for example.
Then, I say, "Thank God for heroes."

But I meet too many men, who say, "I've wrecked my life upon
the rocks of my own unhappiness. Save me. Save me." Well,
I've tried it, Kiddo. It seldom works. Plus, there's rarely a medal
for the heroine, or even a respite from rowing, rowing, rowing
your boat. And, it's very tiring.

How much better for you to save your own life. To come to me, not
grasping and gasping and storm-tossed. To come to me serene and happy
and not needing a thing.

To be called a Saving Grace puffs the ego. But those men with wrecked lives . . .
They wrecked it themselves. Only they can fix it. And they only wind up
resentful that you tried and tried and their life is still in pieces.

Come to me as your equal. Do not ask me to be your savior. Saving yourself
would make you much cuter. Plus, there wouldn't be that lopsided inequality
that makes for so much teeter-tottering and less real exchange.

Now I, for one, consider Grace Darling one of my personal heroes.
However, for the record, I've noted that the brave girl died alone.

August Night

There is a glamour
in the hot summer night
which lazily stretches onward,
that's impossible to summon
in the eternity of winter.
The damp heat is filled with
the warmth of romance,
making cab rides
exquisite adventure.
The air is still
and creates a restlessness.
Evening seems splendorously long.
An undercurrent reminds
that such luxury fleets
and makes this joyful boredom
this rich and singular
sense of wonderment
so preciously perishable.
This heat, this languor
might never be recaptured
on a similar steamy eve.
For tonight is forever
and once spent
gone forevermore.

Assessment

There are things there are no pain pills for:
decisions, loss, regret.

The tumor is out, the body heals
But what caused the malignancy?

If I had been kinder to myself, or others
would something dark have formed inside me?

The choice now, is how I handle insult, or anger, or resentment.
Do I let it chew up my insides?

Does hiding what I will not look at
give long-passed hurt a secret power over me?

How much value will I place on what others think, now?
Now, that I have been granted this reprieve?

We are creatures of habit, yet somehow I am awake and aware.
How will I value every breath?

There are things there are no pain pills for:
decisions, loss, regret.

Ages ago, a divine being said, "Life is suffering."
Ages ago, Mother said, "You must suffer to be beautiful."

Now that I am beautiful, how do I keep this beauty?
It seems I must make friends with the source of my pain.

Since I am acquainted with the author of all my woes
I know where to begin.

Planet Speak

When I met you I thought
You were a little like
(pardon the expression) an asteroid.
You have size, mass, substance—
But since you left the orbit
of a large and lovely planet that . . . disappeared
well, you seem a little adrift to me.

Happy? Yes, you seem to be.
Involved in stellar activities? Oh yes.
But you're the kind that needs a center
a place that you know is home
one that gives you constancy.

I am a beautiful but small planet.
I have a certain stability.
I feel your pull
toward all I am.

Though you are spending your days
with a few random comets
Let me offer you space
and time
and happiness light as air.

I am a beautiful
but small planet.
You are (pardon the expression)
an asteroid.
We were made to be together
and dance in the sky.

Heart in Flight

There is a part of us
that wants to cease to be
to stop struggling each day
and float up to the sky
like a bird with outstretched wings
who knows the secrets of the wind.

We close the heart down
since life can hurt so much.

But to feel a great love
an ecstasy
a vibration
arising deep inside one's breast
the stirring and fluttering of those wings
that still want to know the earth
and feel the joy that life can bring.
I am told it may be worth it again.

Be strong, heart's hummingbird
I am just little.
and these feelings are so big.

Will my heart burst?
or will it whither?
I am battered from the past.
Yet the heart is braver than I know
and wants to fly again.

The Starfish King

I shall meet you
in the sea
under a coral
canopy

We will swim
without a care
Play hide and seek
in lobster's lair

Explore the bay
throughout the day
We'll have our lunch
on a clam shell tray

I'll weave for you
a starfish crown
from oyster beds
where pearls abound

And you will hold
the trident true
made by the faeries
just for you

For you will sooth me
with your smile
and we shall rest
a little while

And you can be
my Starfish King
and in my Mermaid's voice
I'll sing

For we are merry
as can be
and Thursdays
you will sing to me

And we will go
on seahorse rides
on sunny days
in gentle tides

So, come now
be my Starfish King
there's nothing that
you need to bring

Just close your eyes
and joyful be
our thoughts will take us
to the sea

And some day if
we're old and gray
it doesn't have to
be that way

Our starfish kingdom
waits so near
Hold the conch
and you shall hear

Let's swim out to
the tidal pool
and or'e the algae
we shall rule

So come, now
be my Starfish King
and in my Mermaid's voice
I'll sing.

Chapter Six

—⁓⌒⌒⌒⌒⌒⁓—

Self

The Influence of Old Ladies

One was full-blooded Cherokee (I was only three) and she treated our little backyard as if it was a symbol of the whole of nature. Teaching me to really see. And somehow the turtles came and rabbits came and robins came and they were all her friends and visitors. Carrots grew for her and the apple tree yielded enough fruit for a few glorious pies. She taught me all about life in-between laundry and cooking and vacuuming. I didn't know how—she was so old and soon died and she taught me about that, too . . . taking out all the tubes and saying, "Nature says it is my time."

One was Hungarian and came to this country at 14 but had no place to stay because her uncle wanted a boy sent instead (they made more money in the sweatshops) but she found accommodation and worked in the cigar factory with my Grandmother and became her best friend. Later she made garments until she was in her late eighties, finally deciding it might be wise to spend more time tending her garden. Her husband and later her son became mentally ill and she never thought she got a raw deal. She made homemade tomato soup and cookies with recipes from a finishing school she attended in Vienna (when times were good). Her life here was sad, grinding and work-work-work but she was the gentlest and most optimistic person I'd ever met. I don't know how she did that. No one ever gave her a medal or a prize but I did so in my heart.

I hear silly people on TV say uneducated things about old ladies. Like they're not strong and couldn't win at arm wrestling and they move slowly. They dismiss the very thought of them.

To me, old ladies are a Hallowed thing. They know everything and still they are gracious. They do not regard the selfishness and vanity of youth as a crime or aberration. They know it's a part of growing up. Say the word "old ladies," not as a curse, but as a prayer. They do not drop bombs or cause wars. It is because of old ladies that we develop a feeling for civilization, and poetry and God. It is sheer luck to know any of them at all.

Learning to Feel

Forgive my lack of skill
I am clumsy like a months-old baby
struggling, unsure
the door has just been opened
and I have heard that emotions might escape.

I am padded with self-protection
crawling on the carpet alone.
Perhaps I may spite myself
never take those first steps
stay protected in the house
never to feel the windstorm.

I am too old for this.
It's natural for most people
that's how it looks to me.
But I was raised in this house
like a tropical fish in a sheltered box
with the temperature set always at 70 degrees.

There are countless playmates there, outside;
caterpillars, inchworms, the sky
I could play and play
and no one will call me in to supper.

But without the security
of shut doors, closed shutters
bolted locks
will I have the sense to come in out of the rain?
What barricades will protect me?

The sounds in the playground are sweet,
birds calling, squirrels chatter.
Yet I know there are wolves out there
snatching innocents with their jaws
tearing them apart in the woods.

I now cross the threshold tentatively
I could go back.

It is not like inside;
kitchen smells, television sounds
the only things challenging there
are my books.
Yes, they have been my world
and my only transport to the place
I see daily through the window.

But I have been warned against
this outside world with such ferocity.
I am not a bad child.
I had a timid heart. But today
I have the heart of an explorer.

A daffodil laughs at me.
"You old little baby
You dear little child
we will not tell your secrets
to anyone
not even to the moon."

"But beware," she continued.
"There is wildness here.
No one will know if you
walk in the woods.
No one will care.
You can go back into the house
to be safe, and it matters not
except, of course, to you, little one."

Nothing grows without sunlight.
See how I've blossomed?
Still, there are small comforts inside
and big risks out here."

I sit perplexed
the daffodil rustles and waves
stones shine
the earth is warm
mustn't I go in now?
mustn't I?

My teeny little hands
clutch the grass
trying to gain a hold

Is all this too much for me?
What does a baby know of feelings?

In fear, I start to cry.
Hooves noiselessly appear
in front of me.
What manner of beast is this?
It could kill me with a kick.
Oh why did I leave the house?
No one taught me to live out here.
A long neck bends
large brown eyes look at me.

A doe! I know it's a doe
from glossy nature texts.

The door to the house is closed.
Surely I can get back in?

I am a wobbly, naïve baby
with only piles of books for friends
I wish to smell the air at night
lie on a bed of branches
and see the stars.
Yet, I am afraid.

The doe looks at me a long time,
with, I dare to think, compassion.
She nuzzles my hair and says,
"I will show you grace, my dear."

As Butterflies Awaken

I wonder if butterflies ever
regret their caterpillar days—
If they might land on a leaf,
point to their chrysalis and say:
"Had I not spun so many layers
of protection, all this time spent
in the darkness
might not have taken so long."

It seems, to me,
in their world
every moment is new.
These royals wear orange robes
and are called Monarchs
as they are Masters of Themselves.

They take themselves lightly
and head for the sweetest nectar.
I appreciate their meandering path
and endeavor to find and feel
the enchantment in my own.

An Old School Chum

I loved her since
all self-destructive people
are loveable;
cheerfully chipping away at themselves
'til their essence leaks out
sometimes in a flood, usually
in a trickle.

And I, the bleeding heart of a different kind,
tried to stop the pain,
patch the wounds.

So, she tried new ways
sweet smoking her brain like so much meat;
the introduction of chemicals, as if
some startling, scalding substance
could remove the dark spots
bleach them 'til her insides
felt white; pure.

Imagine if they were!
—my school-chum's insides—
not sick with rot
not worn by self-hate.
If, by some miracle
she felt good about herself
clean and whole and
the way she already is
if she would look
deep within to the core
beyond the decay.

If she could see straight through
and know how beautiful she really is
would she have the courage
to stop pulling herself apart?

Or would she just dismiss
all of that self-owned loveliness
as the taunting apparition
of a stranger.

Healing

Get well soon they say.
I do my best to obey.

Small Lessons

Sometimes these are small lessons God has for us.
Like not to push yourself too hard when you are sick.
Or not to always believe that those who love you
want the want the same thing for you
as you want for yourself.

In your mind you know these things.
They are small lessons, like if you don't organize a cabinet
you can't find what's in there.
But you always have to keep it organized all the time.

Repeating, repeating, like not to push myself too hard
I am always pushing myself too hard.
It seems such a small thing I am repeating, but who else
will do the work?

So, last week, for the first time, my dear sweet body
said, "No. Do not push me." It made me feel sad and
helpless.

Such a small lesson I am repeating. Repeating. Repeating.
Sometimes, these are small lessons God has for us.
Sometimes, these small lessons are big.

About Getting a Personnel Job

Am I but this person?—well
I do not know
nor can I tell.
Am I but this person—el—
elegantly appointed to run pell-mell
resplendently rich in
what none could sell
my fearless self?
(you know me, well)
I cannot say, but can I be
this person-el
personnel-ity?
Is this but a
poisoned hell?
Can I tell ?
My person shall
be sentenced into
personnel.
Let us hope this venture
turns out well.
(I shall.)
Am I but this person?
(Time will tell.)

Hap-O-Meter

I've decided not
to gauge the happiness
I have each day
by the amount of attention
you give to me.

Chapter Seven

Hope

Everyday Offerings

I have given you hand-carved wood, the sound of laughter
and the jewel of a constant heart.

You have given me confidence; I had thrown mine out the window
when he left and closed the door.

Stay with me a little. I will make you goulash and be gentle with the spices,
I will button your buttons out of whimsy and unbutton them out of desire.

You will circle your arms around my waist as I do the dishes
and hug me a little while my hands are submerged and occupied
with plates.

After you've gone, I will send you wistful Chinese poetry,
lucky amulets for protection and all my good wishes.

You might send me your photo, a favorite book, and letters
filled with longing.

I will not hint at nor indicate the deeper treasure I would share.

If you want to be with me always, you will find your way home.

When I Spotted the Sheriff

I saw the Sheriff of Nottingham
on a bus, headed for the East Side.

Months ago, at the Renaissance Fair
he smiled at me there
in his forest green tights
and pointed felt hat
he was quite something to look at!

But on the 72nd Street Bus
there were so many between us.
And he was just another
wickedly handsome man
trying to get somewhere in Manhattan.

Oh, wouldst thou be lawless
and willing
in the woods with me?

Beyond Words

After the surgery
I could barely greet you
And said I must sleep.
You said, "rest well," and
opened your book.

Each time I awoke,
for hours and hours
you were relaxed,
turning pages
covering the room
in the warm glow of caring.

Friendship is easy in good times.
But to sit, silently, and to just "be,"
bringing the comfort of who you are
the beauty of your gift nearly brought tears.

Most everyone wishes for the presence of angels
But we humans seem to make so little time
to be present. To sit silently with a friend
and watch over them through a difficult time.

You taught me what people do—
Well, that deeds can be
better than words.
No poem I could write
could match the grace of your actions. Ever.
Thank you.

Not Just Love

I don't *just* love him.
I also have extremely complimentary
things to say
about the ground he walks on.

Feast

Taking my time with the vegetables
cubing each piece into bite-sized savories.
Then, a brush of oil
to make them glisten and shine.
A touch of sea salt
each like a quartz crystal
coaxing out deeper flavor.

And soon, a feathering of fresh dill.
it will make the cucumber salad dance
and will marry the mushrooms and barley.

The main fare is roasting slowly,
its fragrance like a promise fulfilled.

For dessert, it is sweet, ripe, fruit
kissed with sugar
and embraced by sweet cream.

Once you arrive, it will be
just the two of us—
cozy at home.

But, first,
I'll set the table
and light the candles
while I sing a song of you.

Quietum Est Mare Profundum

Water is the source of life.
After this rebirth
I cry like a child.
No emotion, just crying.
Letting the floodgates open
letting all that water go to the source.

Now, with all anew
a tender shoot breaks through the ground.
I cry like a girl.
With some emotion, in a gentle brightening dawn
the seedling has been watered and may grow.

I think of softly raining skies
refreshing an emerald outstretched leaf
and the mist rising like a veil
from an eager lake at dawn.
I cry like a woman.

The past feels healed and finalized.
Sunlight warms my face as I satisfy my thirst.
Nothing dammed up, nothing to release.
Nothing to drown in.
All is flowing, sparkling, out to sea.
And I dare myself to hope.

About You

There might be a poem
in here about you.
There might be eight.
Okay, not eight . . .

I prefer to be mysterious
about who makes me
delirious.

There's something about you
I quite like to see
and you might just appear
on page number 3
and your eyes might intrigue me
on Page 44
My love must you know
j'te'dore?

This urge to be
mysterious
is really, really serious.

No one wants to be in love alone
Especially when we're quite full grown.

So, just for now,
in my own little way
Let me be shy until at least
Saturday
And by then, I might give you a clue
since there' something quite inspiring
About You.

State of Affairs

There is nothing new under the sun
except—Everything.
You smiled at me.

Cherry Blossoms

Each year nature sneaks up on me.
That riot of color
I mean—white, grey and brown for months
and then—pink.
Who but nature would startle so?
Pink! The audacity!
Pink little buds and blooms
ephemeral and lasting no time at all
after a few short—
Then, it's showering pink buds
in your hair.
Who could be in a bad mood?
Who could forget that love exists—
with bits of pink flowers in your hair?

Chapter Eight

Observation

Amateur

How short the skirt
is not an indication
she would be any good
at the art of flirtation.

Country & Western Lament

(sung with appropriate twang a la Mary Kay Place)
((Intro—steel guitar in upbeat instrumental solo. Violin joins in with lyrics))

Tell me why are all the men I meet
married, drunk or gay?
I don't know just what it is
that makes them all this way.
Is there someone just for me?—
I get on my knees and pray.
Oh, why are all the men I meet
married, drunk or gay?

Some Days

I think the only reason
people get married is to
show their ex-lovers that
they have found
someone else at last.

One Ordinary Afternoon

Fifteen years ago when I worked at
The World Trade Center
I remember my secretary telling me
someone was calling me from the Concorde—
Did I want to pick up the phone?
It was very exciting.
I knew you weren't the right guy
but I answered anyway.
I liked you, respected you
I couldn't replace your wife, who
felt so neglected for so long,
she took lots of money and went to
find someone who could pay more attention.
I felt sad for you.
You still loved her.
And though I was sorely tempted
there was no second date.
I look back now and see
there's no more World Trade Center
there's no more Concorde
the company you sacrificed a wife for
got swallowed in a takeover bid
and I'm not sure even, if you still walk the earth.
I realize each day, more than ever
There are no ordinary afternoons.

Vermin and the Vexed/Confessions of a Former Network TV Newswriter or

(Why do people loooove celebrities?)

It's my job, you see,
writing the news.
Detailing the events,
the victims, the interviews.

Here's the rock star, the accused,
the hot girl on TV,
"Tell us about your poor childhood…
Your adult ennui…"

I describe the spectral lives
of the vermin and the vexed.
And feeling close to neither,
wonder privately why anyone
is interested in either.

Ode To A Tomato

Thump, thump, squish.
I liked you better
in your prime.

Hollywood Retro

When I think of the charm
of the classic film actor
a Fedora hat is definitely a factor.

Some of them looked better you know
wearing a dashing tilted chapeau

Even in today's films
or in the days of olden,
you couldn't get
much better looking
than William Holden.
And in some of the films
Mr. Holden would make,
a Fedora hat was icing on the cake

Hats made men look solid
—keen and authoritative.
Fedoras improved the look
of any Hollywood native

In those days even eeling
reporters looked best
with a card in the band of their
hats marked "Press"

Males Mitchum, Bogart
all the first-at-bats
showed a come-hither style
in their Fedora hats

And I dream of the day
Well, I wish it could be now
when men will start to crease
the brim above their brow

And though some think lids
are best if they're sat on
Don't believe them, Dear
and please, leave your hat on

No One Ever Said It Was Easy

I don't love him
when I'm with him.
But I seem to need him
when he's not with me.

Reflection Pond

Glittering mirrors of golden light
dance excitedly
while the rest of the pond seems still.
It isn't.
A white crane spots a fish below
and knows he's found his dinner.
A turtle pokes his head out and soon
his flippers swim gracefully toward
a half-sunken branch.
A dragonfly seems indecisive
and does not pause to rest.
The natural world moves forward.
Each part of creation at its own pace.
Yet I am stuck on you.

Kissing

You are always kissing me.
I've thought about
making a report to the
local Kissing Authorities.

They will ask:
"What have you to declare?"
And I will proclaim:
"Utter Happiness."

Chapter Nine

Longing

A Poem For My Beloved

I long for you.
Every time I see something glimmering with grace, there you are.
I've walked through a rain of falling cherry blossoms,
spinning like confetti on a breezy day.
Horseshoe crabs were dancing in the waves,
locked together in the undertow, while seagulls, aloft and lonely
shrieked and cried.
Irises blossomed a special shade of periwinkle.
Sunsets arranged a revolving spectacle in your honor.
The fragrance of blooming honeysuckle called to me as I walked.
All these things happened for you.
I wanted to turn to you, show you, kiss your neck for no reason.
I long for you.
Did I remember to say that I love you?

Inside A Girl's Sewing Basket

I bought a box of antiques at the auction.
among the jumble
a tiny Chinese sewing basket looked interesting
a turquoise blue Peking glass handle
and one ancient coin, dangled on top as decoration.
Inside the round woven case
was the real treasure. Five beautiful seashells
and a photo of a young man in uniform.
Was he someone's Daddy?
Or some young girl's brother?
What happened to him in the war?

Was that the best day they ever had together?
Walking the beach, talking, laughing, collecting seashells.
It was breezy that day, but beautiful.
Not too many shells, so each seemed a delicate gift.
Sometimes one would strike his fancy and he'd hand it to her.
Sometimes she would pick one herself.
It wasn't the shells themselves. It was the sunlight
and the closeness and the feeling of time being short.
A day worth keeping.
A day she tried to bring back, looking at the picture,
touching the shells.
With so many feelings, she shut them in a basket.
Life could have been different, if.
The basket and shells remained, a tribute to memory
marking that day for some 50 years
till they could no longer stay in her keeping.
No scavenger, no collector of beautiful items
could ever know the value set upon this stored treasure.
Priceless to her, I got it for ten dollars.
And wondered how memory can be heavier and lighter than
the pull and shift of tides.

My Comforter

Who will take my hand
when it's time to go
if all my friends have gone?

When all that's left is a worn-out shell
and there's nothing more left to leave?
I've heard the stories
that love comes 'round
that it shines knowingly in our eyes

That we brighten up when we know it's near
and familiar voices whisper
we should have no fear.

When the new path begins to unfold
will yours be the hand that I hold?
Will you stop what you are doing
in Heavenly climes
and remember this good friend
from previous times?

It is a great comfort to know
there are guides who will gently bestow
the presence of goodness
the compass of truth
the forgiveness of the errs
of vanity and youth
who softly remind us
to our endless surprise
the love in our hearts – it never dies

and whoever the handholder will be
well, bless them for coming for me.

Request for a Gift

———∿∿∽∘∾∾↶⟲↷∾∿∘∿∿———

I miss you.
I dream of the day
you will cross the ocean
to come and see me.

We can go to a restaurant
and sit across from each other.
I will look into your eyes
and forget what I was talking about.

How could I ever ask for more than this?

My Unobtainable Object

You have this knack for making
every moment with you delicious.
I savor each morsel of time we share.
Why can't you just be a jerk?

The Gardener's Song

If all the dear ones
in the land
were but flowers
in my hand

I'd place you singly
on a shelf
and let you see
my inner self

If you were sea
and I was air
I'd kiss you gently
everywhere

But you are man
and made of skin
you build-up walls
and hide within

My love I prove
your love: denied
Some have small hearts
compared with pride

But if you were
a single bloom
you'd scent the air
and douse my gloom

For blossoms spend
such happy hours
Who ever heard
of lovesick flowers?

Still we are both
in human form
my tend'rest wish
to keep you warm

Because you have
a human face
my eyes still call
for your embrace

If all the dear ones
in the land
were but flowers
in my hand

I'd hold you close
in quiet mirth
'til I grew roots
into the earth.

God's Full Attention

Some parents have small attention spans
I was important for short periods of time
and somehow my mind thought
my good grades, my good looks, my good behavior
weren't terribly interesting. That the neighbor's cat,
the baby across the aisle in the restaurant, the
repair bill for the car, were all vying to steal from me
what I needed.

Silly me.

I did not realize how someone is—is just how they are.
I saw it as something wrong with me—That nothing I did
was ever worthy.

Then one day, a great Saint came to New York City
And she looked at me. Paid attention to me.
Ripped my thoughts into shreds and laughed.
I knelt in rapture, first uncomfortable with her gaze
then wanting to run, afraid of the spotlight.
Instead I inhaled and relaxed, into the Ahhhhhhhhhh.

In that moment, I realized I had God's Full Attention.
In that moment, I realized I always did.
Bless you, my parents. All Parents. Bless All Great Teachers.
Some lessons take nearly a lifetime to learn.

I want to give you this gift if you are missing it like I was.
So, now, let's tell everybody the secret.
You have God's Full Attention, too.

What I Miss

It's not the part in 1940's movies where
the music swells as the loving couple embraces. (fade to black)
It's how you joyfully taught me to dance the two-step
since I had never learned.
It's how you packed my suitcase that traveling day
when my clothes would not leave you. They were depressed
and unruly and would not fold-up properly. You soothed them,
smoothing every wrinkle, coaxing them back into place
as they cried. You did that for me.
The sound of your voice has its own music. Intimate and tender
and glorious to my ear. Still, yes. It is still song to me.
Oh, maybe how you get jealous a little (just a little)
When other men think I'm pretty. I love that you're a fool.
Don't you know they can never be you?
It's not the part in the 1940's movies . . .
Oh. All Right. It's that too.

Chapter Ten

———⌇⌇◦⟨⊱⊙⊰⟩◦⌇⌇———

Joy

Our World

The world is filled with consideration.
I have proof.
For when I kiss my darling
the world goes away
and takes its cares along.

You wonderful world!
Because of you
I get to kiss my darling.

He walks through the door
and while kissing him on tiptoe
I close my eyes
and get to peek at Heaven.

Valentine's Day

A celebrated date
to osculate
your mate.

The Poet on Vacation

The ocean heaves and churns,
rocks tumble in the undertow.

I should be polishing words.

Palm trees sway, creating
the mildest rustle in the air.

I should be editing, making
fewer lines seem like many.

I begin to feel hungry
Is it for food?

There's never normally time to write,
is there? They drain you dry at work
and sometimes, once home, I can only
manage terse verse.

The sun is shining brilliantly.

Yet other days, those beautiful days when
all flows, there really should be more of
those. Red letter days. With blue and gold
and conch shell pink!

The girl on the beach wants a kiss.
The girl on the beach gets a kiss.

The Week I Learned To Trust

Happiness crept in to my bed
and I wanted to push him away
I was certain he'd never stay
and I, too proud to go looking for him
or ever to mourn his loss
gave him a kick.
But he, too fast for me
only came closer
and kissed my tears away.

Love Poem

I do not know what to say of what love means.
I only know, what my one love, can mean to me.
His very existence
assigns value to the contents of the globe.

Smoocher's Delight

Won't you be my Smoocher-ooo.
My Cuddly-Wuddly rendezvous?
A hidden wink
before we blink
and wishes could come true.
If you'll be my oodle-y coodle-y smoocher-ooo.

Will you be my Honey-bear?
Hold my hand at county fair?
A little *kiss* and more of *this* . . .
You never would be blue.
If you'll be my scoobey-doobie smoocheroo.

Won't you be my Sweetie-keen?
The bestest one I've ever seen—
My cozey-woah-zee never dozey
one so sweet and true?
If you'll be my huggy-wuggy smoocheroo.

If you'll be my Candy Drops
we'd lunch all day on lollipops.
We'd skate and date and stay up late
and dance the boogaloo.
If you'll be my eubie-woobie smoocheroo.

My Fancy Dancing Prancing Heart

After being on the shelf for so long
My heart wants to put on a vainglorious display
like a Lipizzaner mare, with a fancy head dress
Theda Bara-style, strutting and trotting and looking
fit and beautiful and making the audience gasp
with praise and appreciation.

My heart wants to fly through the air
like a trapeze show beauty, awesome and limber and
balanced on the swing with
both arms reaching toward heaven,
perfectly capable of making her greatest catch.

This heart of mine wants to rush forward and leap
like the finest and fastest of long distance runners,
outpacing all the rest in my
display of stamina and fortitude and . . . heart.

I am blowing the dust off of you, my precious heart.
Move a bit forward at your own pace, little one.
I know you have big ideas, and you are sometimes timid.
But this is finally your time, my sweet heart.
You can do anything, now.
Let's go out there like a champion.

A Present From You

I've spent my whole life liking people
but feeling somehow apart from them.
Then, we met and you handed me
an invitation.
It read: "Welcome to the world."
A simple thing; yet it opened up
not just the world, but the universe.

A Laurel

What type of flower for you
when only the most memorable will do?
Should I start with . . .
anemones?—we're not enemies
A hydrangea?—you're no stranger.
A rose to ease your woes?
A geranium for your cute cranium.
Will a pansy suit your fancy?
How would you chose
were you in my shoes?
Would some phlox knock off your sox?
Would lilies be quite silly?
Would a daisy drive you crazy?
Does your heart skip
over parrot tulips?
I'll pick chose them all, you know
with a little card
and a great big bow.
So here's the bouquet I've assembled to amaze.
I'm just hoping there is a big enough vase!

Chapter Eleven

A Place That Is Ours

My "If Only"

Are you out strolling
with Johnny Walker?
I love you anyway.

Are you singing in your beer?
changing history?
or teaching dervishes
the ecstasy
of whirling?
How you leave me breathless.

You are my BIG LOVE.
You are my "If only . . ."
You are my waking thought
my bittersweet smile
the root of my kindness
my lightheartedness
and my most serious wish.

You are the sun
yet I burn for you.

The Facts About Amelia Earhart

The newspaper said today, after decades of searching
they found Amelia Earhart's plane.
She and her navigator were
blown off the charts, out of the sky
and in to love, or so a wonderful novel
once suggested.

Was there ever such a place
they inhabited
where two people who knew themselves
could meet each other?

Did she decorate the navigator's hair
with seashells? Did she fashion little umbrellas
for their libations from sea urchin spines and palm leaf?

Did he bring her such fruits
tasting of cool rain and sweet breezes?
Did he sing the songs of the sea in her ear
as they danced near the twinkling evening waters?

Perhaps she was holding a tropical flower
when she realized she had become a mystery
the modern world could not solve.

In my dream of dear Amelia,
she learned to fly without wings
and he charted for her a starry path
to territories beyond the clouds.

(Noted aviatrix Amelia Earhart disappeared with her navigator, Fred Noonan, over the
Pacific Ocean during their attempted around-the-world flight in 1937. In August 2012,
news reports speculated that remains of her airplane may have finally been found.)

Ivory Crisp Dream

I was twelve
and had a crush
on a homosexual
English teacher
who carried a purse.
(He called it a man-bag.)
We read "Romeo and Juliet"
aloud in class that term
and, I, as teacher's pet
was <u>always</u> allowed to be Juliet
and everyone else took turns
being everyone else.

Last year, the English teacher
didn't like me. She always put
"handwriting needs improvement"
in the margins with lots of !!!!!

Sasha Freedman, who writes
endless stories about her dog
but has big, bold, perfectly-formed
script . . . . She always got A's.

Now, <u>I</u> do!
and I love my teacher
because he cares about
what's inside of things
and he takes the time to look.
I really like some Shakespeare now
(but not as much as Mr. G.)

I love stories and
words and what things mean
and most of all
I love F. Scott Fitzgerald
because he knows something
I feel in my heart
and can't explain to my parents.

He is a romantic figure
in my life;
reckless and talented and tragic.
This year is my first time being
teacher's pet.
A definite improvement.
Two grades ago
I was given the silent treatment
(all year!)
by our small, private-school class
because
the Headmistress' daughter doesn't
like me, either.
(I still won't do as she says!)
and, I don't like sports.
That teacher, she stayed quiet.
Her hair was mostly white
and her favorite word was
"retirement."

One day, last month
Mr. G. brought in a stack of
typed paper—a manuscript he wrote.
He said (in front of the whole
class) "Scout can see this
but no one else. She's the only one
with clean hands."
I am twelve and I have power.

Mr. G says I am a good writer
and that's why I am his favorite.
My words, which once brought me
silence
now bring me love!

When I sleep at night
my father's not ill
I am not awkward
and everything is
beige and floating.
I have an
Ivory Crisp Dream
that says:
"You love to write
and writing loves you.
This feeling writing gives you
can always stay in your heart."
When the world is light-light
beige and floating
some things are clear
love is clear . . . and solid . . . and in focus.
It is the color of French Vanilla ice cream,
white chocolate . . . and possibly Heaven.

Father's health gets worse.
He suffered so quietly.
I want to go to boarding school
and be just like Haley Mills.
(She smokes cigars in the boiler room
in the beginning of the movie, when nobody
likes her and in the end, everyone likes her and
they cry because she decides to be a nun.)

Mom and I see Mr. G in the discount store
buying music, and she tells him,
"Scout won't be coming back to your
school in the fall. She's won a scholarship
to a highly-rated out-of-state school."
Mr. G stands back and swallows air and says,
"Why not a school for the arts? Your child has
such a dramatic flair."
Mom shakes her head and says,
We're not that kind of family."

And I go to bed every night.
Sometimes I think about
F. Scott Fitzgerald and
people wearing very beautiful clothes
and longing for things
on jewel-green summer lawns.
(Not the kind we have in New Jersey.)

And when I am very lucky
things are cream-colored
and calm
and words and love
and yearning
float effortlessly by on clouds.
In my Ivory Crisp Dream
I am twelve yet
I am not twelve.
I am the world's most
famous and glamorous
actress and writer and
Haley Mills' best friend.
F. Scott Fitzgerald
invites us to parties
where we wear hats
while sipping iced tea
and the world is
a kind, benevolent beige.

The Old Man

Do you think all I am
is a fragile sack of bones
in an ill-fitting shirt?

Do you look at my
watery blue eyes
and start to count
the crisscross of lines
across my face?

Remember me
climbing a tree.

Can you tell I was
good at sports?
a likeable boy?
protective of my mother?
I'd pick daisies for her in the field.
She had so few joys.

I always loved trees
how their branches held the sky.
When I was eight, I fell out of one
and broke a bone.
Had to climb with one hand
for a while.

Remember me
climbing a tree.

When I met Susan
she teased me about my long legs
of course we married
she was complicated
and tried to be on my side.

Something terrible passed
between us once
that was my lowest day—
something I never expected.
Her forgiveness was the best thing
that ever happened to me.
But I didn't know it at the time.

I loved her
more than I
ever imagined I could
and I'd bring her flowers
to remind her
my love for her
was always blooming.

Remember me
climbing a tree.

I wonder how God judges a man
by what he does in life?
I think he takes the best and worst
and tosses 'em out the window so
all that remains is middle.

Wouldn't we all do things differently?
More slowly, too.

I wish I had kissed my wife more.
I did not know her days were short
and thought there was time enough for kissing.

I would have wiggled my toes in mud
without guilt
and helped more turtles safely across
the road.

I would not have been so precise
about returning to work on time
after lunch break.
I would have tasted food more.

I wish I had helped more folks
along the way and not worried about
what it looked like to other people.

I wish I had turned more ordinary Wednesdays
into special days to celebrate.

The kindnesses. Taking time
to listen. I think He counts them
like gold coins and banks them against
all the debts of sadness a man creates.

Remember me
climbing a tree
the bringer of bouquets
the boy, for fun
would jump and run
the man; loved holidays.

Remember me
climbing a tree.

What If?

There's a moment sometimes
when I hear a bittersweet song
and your faces pokes into my thoughts.

It's been years.
Years!

They say I'm a different person now.
But the love that was, that is
it's love. So it doesn't think of stopping.

If I wrote songs
Yours would be called, "What if?"

I would clear the desk top
and open fresh, clean paper
I would start by laughing
and thinking of your charm.

I would write of tenderness and grace
of feeling entirely special and astonished
I would say truthfully, that I always thought
You were the one for me.

After, when fate intervened
I would tell of feeling all at sea
storm-tossed and alone.

I would tell of not wanting to go on
but going on anyway.

Later, I would crumple the salty pages
And again, start afresh.

And then, to bless us both
I would take out
all the sad parts.
There have been
enough sad parts already.

And love, well, it's love.
I want the heart of that
transcendent place to be
all either of us can remember.

Does Living in New Jersey Bring You More or Less Love?

(Post-Hurricane Sandy thoughts)

I used to think
with all the traffic
-the busy citizens,
Maybe, it could be less.
That in order to find what I needed,
I'd have to travel to New York City
to some alienating bar where things wouldn't seem
to work, either.

Since Jersey is always the butt of jokes-
Where could love live?
Where *could* it live?
in laughter?
in the heart?
in the inner being
of the most populated
most welcoming state?

Maybe, that's what hearts should be—.
populated with warm welcome.

In Jersey, we are
crammed, jammed, pushed up
so closely to each other.
And yet, greeting strangers kindly
accepting our differences
offering to help through challenges.
I have found a not-so hidden
current of love in New Jersey.

That's the state's real official secret
Our *inner* state.

So, maybe my heart
is in the right place after all.

My Friend's World

This side of the Borbetian Galaxy
somewhere between the Truth
and a mournfully blowing train whistle
there is you.
The writer who does not need to write
because it is ALL inside him.

The World-Series winning ballplayer.
The slim shark out-cueing Minnesota Fats.
The Heavyweight Champion of the World
who does not believe in violence
so he never fights.
If you've done these things
1,000 times in your head,
they must be true.

For this is a Galaxy of Kindness.
Where Johnny Mize and Mickey Mantle
show up to play catch with the neighborhood kids
and with the neighborhood kids-at-heart
so no one is left out.

Where Brando regularly haunts
the Woodside Diner
and casually chats
to the locals
about "On the Waterfront"
while wearing stylish chinos.

Some of us create a wonderful world
to take the place of all of the shoulds.

In this rare and gentle galaxy
open a novel at the library on 42nd Street
and someone's ashes may fall out
because they don't want to leave
their favorite books.

Comely barmaids serve tea and cookies
and tell stories of their homeland
while reciting treasured poems.

The only argument is over the bill
for everyone wants to treat
and the one who gets the check
overtips by 25%

I know this is
only one of your worlds
and everyone else lives in it.

But there are some parts
that the rest of us ordinary citizens
dearly appreciate.

Aftermaths of Soft Septembers

There will be other mouths to kiss
and I will shed tears in future
over men I do not yet know.

But you are the one who recognized me
the way birds know their own kind
the way mariners pick a star in the sky
and never lose sight of it.

You subtly permeate
all contacts with the outside world
your memory—a skilled thief—has stolen
all the superlatives
and left me quite surprised.
Was I sleeping at my post?

There are some years left to life
and during the milestone days
that mark each one's passing
I will not be able to stop reflecting
on all the chances and consequences
that could have brought us more time together.

When I am old
I will have convinced myself
I was being silly about you
that no man could ever have had
all those dear qualities I attribute to you.
I will be wrong.

Chapter Twelve

Higher Love

Humanity

When you say, "What can I do?
After all, I am only human."
Stand tall.
Relax in your body a bit.
Contemplate these qualities:
Buddha's determination to eliminate the suffering of all
Christ's compassion for his murderers
Solomon's trust that people will do the right thing
Mother Teresa's vision to see the poor and sick as worthy
Ann Frank's hope that good will triumph
Jackie Robinson's belief in himself and others
Stephen Hawking's limitless nature, as he ponders the infinite.
So what can you do?
After all, being human means you have access to greatness
inside your very own heart.

The Buddha of the Holland Tunnel

(A True Story of What Remains)

———⌒∽◦⌒◦⊙◦⌒◦∽⌒———

A few weeks after the World Trade Center fell
A friend's wife told him
"Take her to the city.
Bring the kid.
Our friend should go back there.
Just don't stay long."
So we went to Manhattan
but nowhere near the destruction.
We went to a Buddhist tea house.
I met a nun.
We had tea.
The kid got restless.
We decided to go home.
A few blocks before the Holland Tunnel
we stopped at a parking space
in front of an antiques store.
The kid wanted a hot dog.
He saw a vendor around the corner.
To kill time, I got out to look in the window.
He was six feet tall, and handsome.
Carved, wooden, confident. God.
Buddha in all his glory.
He looked like he owned the store.
I looked harder.
For the first time not thinking of my friends.
Then, thinking of my friends.
How can people disappear?
Buildings crumble?
How much hate does it take to fly a plane
Into . . . ?

I saw the Buddha.
It got so silent.
He showed me a thousand years.
He showed me thousands of years.
He showed me war, hope.
He showed me birth and human heartache.
He showed me my pain was nothing new to any generation.
He asked me what remains.
I didn't understand.
He asked me what remains after 1,000 years.
What remains after thousands of years?
He indicated, gesturing so I would think . . . and finally . . .
Nothing of human hands
only of human heart.
Love is all that remains.

We sat in the car.
Mustard got on the seat.
I thought about that handsome prince
In the store window, for a long time.
Two years later, I called that antiques shop.
Was the Buddha still there?
I wanted it at any price.
By some miracle could I afford it?
I described the glowing
wooden figure to the manager
hoping that particular Buddha
wasn't everyone's taste.
Maybe he was in the back, in a dusty corner?
My description was perfect

"He was larger than life.
Gorgeous. Inspiring.
The statue seemed alive.
The most beautiful one I'd ever seen."
"Sorry," said the manager.
"We've never had anything like that in here."

God Speaks in Birds

A friend told me the other day that she's sure
God speaks in birds.
She's lucky, and I'm lucky, too, since
Yes, I know this.
Like the way the cardinal appears in
the birch tree Dad and I planted.
It's *him*, of course, coming and laughing
the day an engagement to
someone just plain wrong for me went kaput
or on my birthday, and even on Christmas morning.
The red, red cardinal male, talking his tinny language
but I know he's chirping love right at me.
Robins symbolize friends who seem mousey but
have a fire in their breast. They could be here or in
the otherworld, but robins mean friendship.
Blue jays are beautiful friends who are still learning to
use their voice. Friends who squawk and can be loud.
and they come to visit, still.
But today, in front of the mall, a falcon—flying low
ten feet off the ground, swooped in front of my car and
I yelled "Wow!, Wow!, Wow!"
Steve Jobs last words
but also my spontaneous living ones
to describe such splendor.
I was alone but had to tell the air.
The surprise of beauty. The reconnection of family and
friends whom I can no longer telephone.
Yes, my friend, God speaks in birds.
And the conversation feels like just the beginning.

After the Siren's Song

Having listened to the forbidden music
Did Jason's ears have a new appreciation
for what they heard?
-The clattering of dinner plates as they are washed.
-The snorting of horses, when they are restless to move.
-The unceasing play of water against the boat.
-The deep exhale before a painful truth.

I'd like to think that after Jason
entered that rarified club
he did not yearn for more
of what could clearly drive him mad.
I'd like to think
that any sound
-a nagging cough
-a ship lad's stutter
entered the realm of music to him.

That all sound became lace-like and
beautiful.
That he gained a deep knowing
of his bountiful good fortune
and that this drove him on
to the greater glories before him.

Laundry Day

When I heard it could be serious
I told the Wise Woman. She said:
"Dear Heart, every day you take off
your clothes, do they weep for being shed?

Who you are always remains.

If it must be, all you are losing
is a costume, which you have
dropped a thousand times before."

Dear One, when the time comes
for new raiment,
my prayer is that you will find me
and recognize me inside my new garments.

Remembering

I could see God in a leaf
a rock
a feather.
I could recognize
the spark of creation
in other people.
But not in myself.
How much I forgot
since the time we were all gathered together.

You don't feel "good enough."
Yet you exist!
You were fashioned
by an artisan's hand.
I can see God in you.
Please!
Know the wonder in yourself.

The Bargain

I gave God my heart since
I thought it was no use to me anymore
and, in the giving, I might be able
to find peace.
God looked at me and smiled.
She reached out to accept the gift
and lit it aflame.

And now a heart
that I used to think had no purpose . . .
Well, it dreams and longs like a teenager.
It wails like a baby.
It grieves like an elderly survivor.
It leaps when it sees beauty.
It moves to the rhythms of the earth.
It fully functions.

I thought I was giving God something worthless
but all I owned.
God gave me back vulnerability
strength, tears, and sweetness.

Oh, watch what you ask for
when you bargain with God.
Since God, being God, always
gives a greater gift.

What They Never Said

(The Healing Poem)

Your mother never told you.
Your father might have hinted at it;

But that was long ago
and you were so young,
he probably thought you knew.
Your lovers never told you.
Don't blame them.
They were afraid that saying it
would make them weak.

Since you were never told

I will tell you.

You are blessed.
You are loved.
You are as wondrous as the design
on a peacock's feather.
You are desirable; as touchable
as rose petals.
You are silk and steel
water and fire.

Do not think you are nothing.
You are everything!

Now that you know the truth,
keep this paper and look at it.
You should have heard this all along
I never want you to forget.

Ecstasy

The rescuer saved the little girl.
Everything is going to be all right.
I passed the test!
He loves me.
No one got hurt.
She cares.
It's here!
We made it.
Good triumphed over evil.
We proved the doctors wrong! The results are clear!
I got first prize.
It's really mine!

As good as it gets, there's more.
No matter what I did, God loves me.
       No matter what!!!

That's cray-zee, that kind of love.
That kind of love that says
"All is forgiven" every single moment.
That's crazy.
Maybe crazy love, but real.
In New York they don't believe this.
they think it's delusional.
Nah-uuugh.
Read enough, learn enough, know enough.
You know what you find out?
It's not where you were looking.

Then one day a hint. Then another.
If you're brave enough to enter the cave of your heart
You find it's in there.

That's what I know, truly, that's what I have.
That love that tells me
I am loved beyond my age, my looks, my character
my brains, my abilities, my possessions.

What I've done or haven't done.
I am loved because I am loved.
The light inside of us is *that* great.

You want love? It's there *inside* you.
Think about it. Feel it. It makes you
so happy you could burst.
No matter what happens.
It's there.
That's ecstasy.

About the Author

Author Terry Benczik has enjoyed a lifelong love of poetry and writing. At 24, she was hired as a full-time staff news writer for CBS News, writing for "Nightwatch," and later for "The CBS Morning News." After CBS, a desire to make a difference brought her into government service, working in offices at the World Trade Center (WTC). She was part of a team that won the New York PRSA's Big Apple Award for their work with international media following the WTC bombing in 1993. She brought reporters on tours of the explosion site and connected them with those who were protecting and rebuilding the damaged areas. Ms. Benczik's essay on her experience the morning of the 2001 World Trade Center attacks was selected by the Library of Congress for the "American Memory" exhibit. Teaching material based on her story was developed by the Library of Congress for classroom use. Ms. Benczik's essay on the George Washington Bridge is in the book "Perpetual Motion," and her essay on the Holland Tunnel is in "Today's Public Relations," by Heath and Coombs. Terry is acknowledged in seven other books including "American Television Drama," by Dr. William Hawes; and in "The Remorseful Day," by Inspector Morse creator Colin Dexter. In 2007, she won a silver medal in Poetry.com's International Poetry Contest. An avid beachcomber, classic film buff, and appreciator of the arts, Ms. Benczik lives in New Brunswick, New Jersey, with a few prized seashells and many, many books.

Made in the USA
Lexington, KY
28 September 2013